SIMPLE TECHNOLOGY

# LEVERS

Liz Lennon and Ellie O'Shea

WINDMILL BOOKS

Published in 2026 by Windmill Books,
an Imprint of Rosen Publishing
2544 Clinton St.
Buffalo, NY 14224

First published in Great Britain in 2023 by Wayland


Editor: Sarah Peutrill
Designer: Lisa Peacock
Science consultant: Peter Riley

Cataloging-in-Publication Data
Names: Lennon, Liz, author. | O'Shea, Ellie, illustrator.
Title: Levers / by Liz Lennon , illustrated by Ellie O'Shea.
Description: Buffalo, NY : Windmill Books, 2026. | Series: Simple technology | Includes glossary and index.
Identifiers: ISBN 9781725397040 (pbk.) | ISBN 9781725397057 (library bound) | ISBN 9781725397064 (ebook)
Subjects: LCSH: Levers--Juvenile literature.
Classification: LCC TJ207.L46 2026 | DDC 621.8--dc23



Printed in China

CPSIA Compliance Information: Batch #QW26WM
For Further Information contact Rosen Publishing at 1-800-237-9932

# CONTENTS

# WHAT IS A LEVER?

When you get up in the morning, do you open a door or switch on a light? If you do, you are using a lever.

There are different sorts of levers that can do different things. What they have in common is that they are all machines!

There are six levers in this picture. Read on in this book and come back to see if you spotted them all.

# FORCES AND MACHINES

A force is a push or pull.

A machine is anything which helps us by taking a force and transferring it to where it is needed.

A lever is a machine that reduces the amount of force needed to move an object or lift a load.

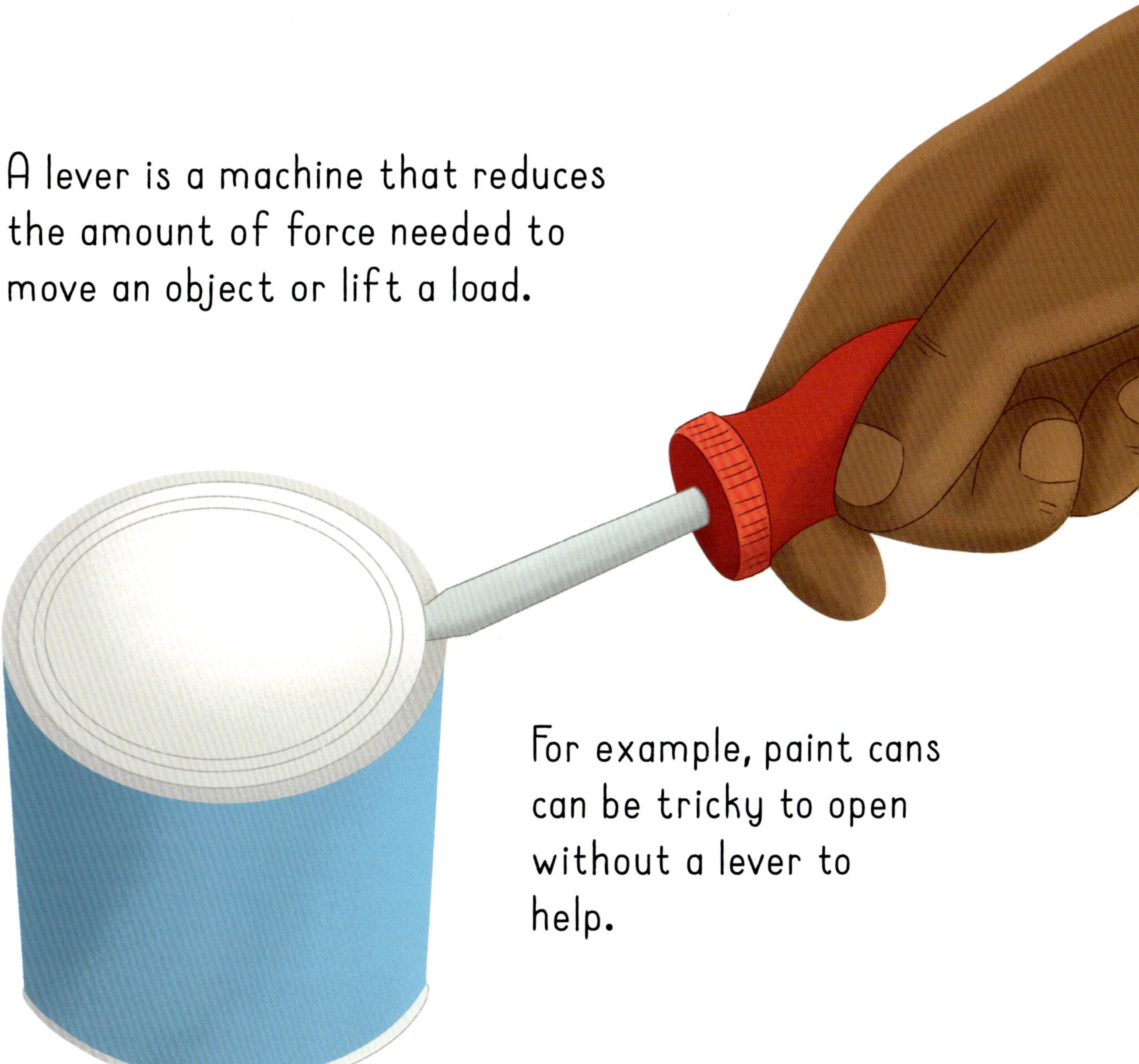

For example, paint cans can be tricky to open without a lever to help.

# THE PARTS OF A LEVER

A lever has three parts.

Fulcrum – the lever turns on the fulcrum and lifts the load. It is also called the pivot.

Load – this is the part that the lever moves

Effort – the force you apply to one end of the lever is the effort

# LIFTING THE LOAD

Can you lift your friend in the air and hold them there easily on your own? Probably not.

With a see-saw you can! A see-saw is a type of lever. It is a plank that tilts on a pivot – its fulcrum.

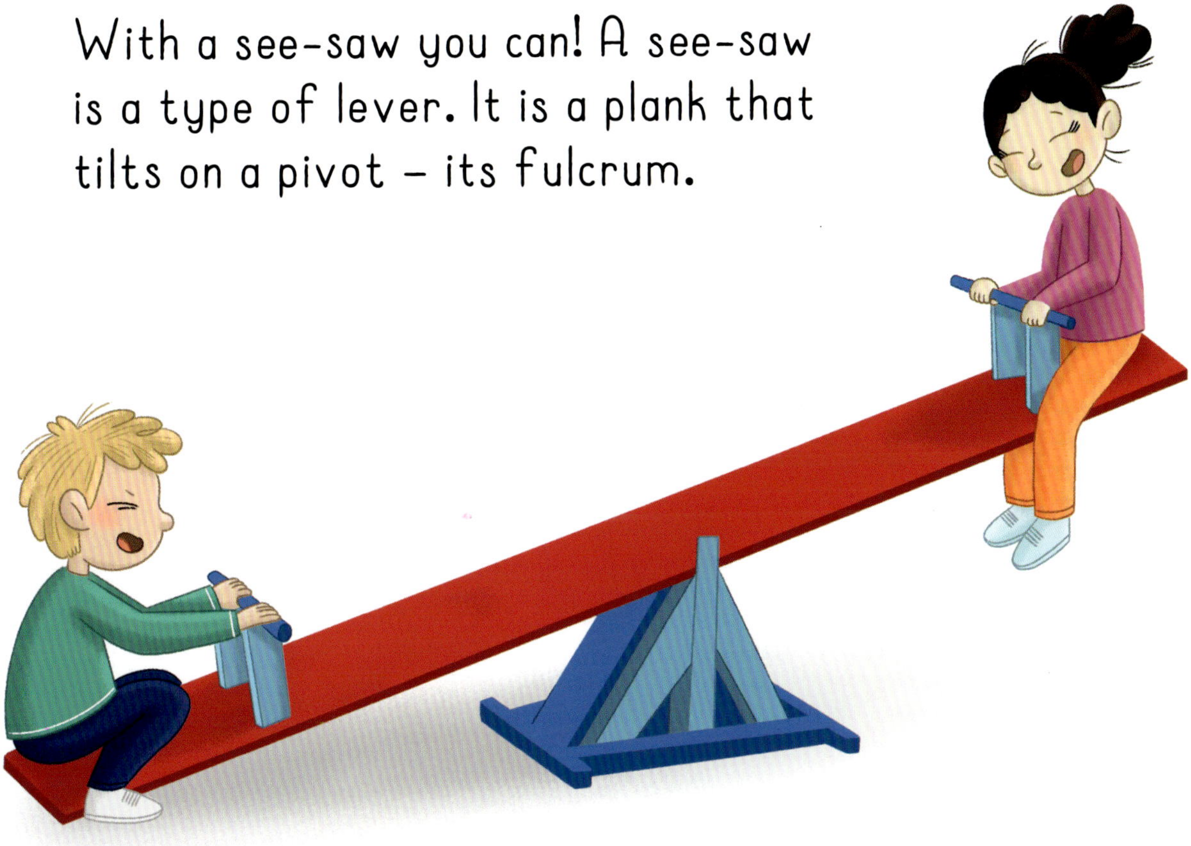

When you push down on one end, the other end goes up!

# MOVING THE FULCRUM

These children have made a see-saw with a piece of wood and a brick.

Look what happens if two children sit at one end.

Now they have moved the brick (the fulcrum).

Can you see what has happened?

A light weight can lift a heavy weight if the heavy weight is near to the fulcrum.

# LIFT OFF

This box is too heavy to lift, but Ryan has an idea! He has found a useful plank.

Ryan slots the plank in under the box, on top of some bricks.

He presses down on the top end of the stick. Now the bottom end is forced up, making the box move. The plank is a lever.

# BIG SHOVEL, LITTLE SHOVEL

Levers can be different shapes and sizes. A shovel is a lever.

The bottom of the shovel first slices its way into sand.

Then the sand surface acts as a fulcrum. Your hands are the effort.

Have you noticed that if you have a shovel with a longer handle, it is easier to lift more sand?

That is because the effort is magnified by the length of the handle.

# WHEELBARROW

A wheelbarrow may not look like a lever, but it is. The wheel acts as the fulcrum and you put the load in the middle.

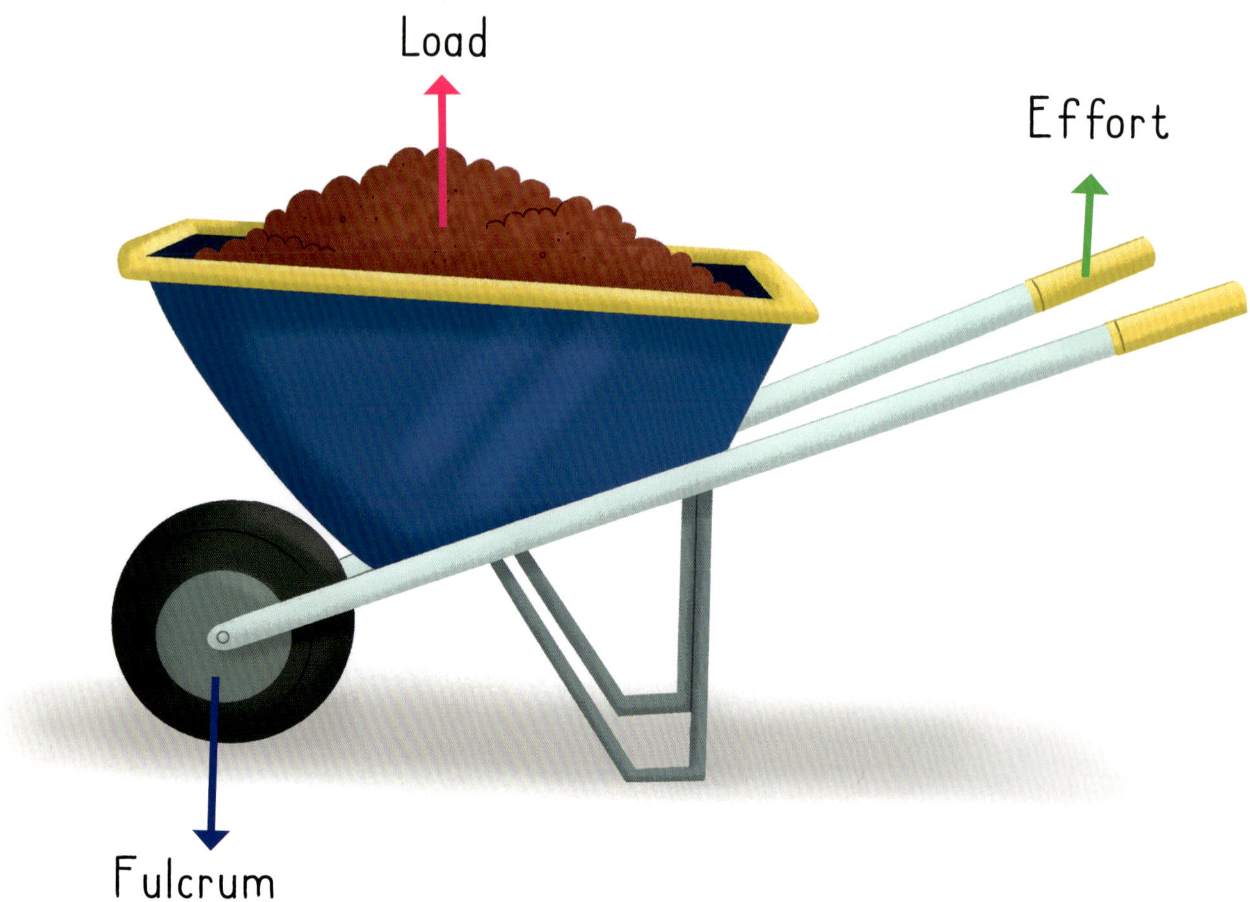

When you lift up the handles (the force), you can move a heavy load easily.

# HAMMER

When a hammer is used to hit a nail, the fulcrum is the user's wrist.

The load is the toughness of the wood stopping the nail going in.

The hammer head is heavy which means that another force, called gravity, adds to the user's muscle force.

# TENNIS RACKET

Sports equipment like bats, golf clubs, and tennis rackets are also levers.

When you hit a ball with a tennis racket, your wrist is the fulcrum. The head of the racket moves much farther than your hand, sending the ball (the load) flying through the air.

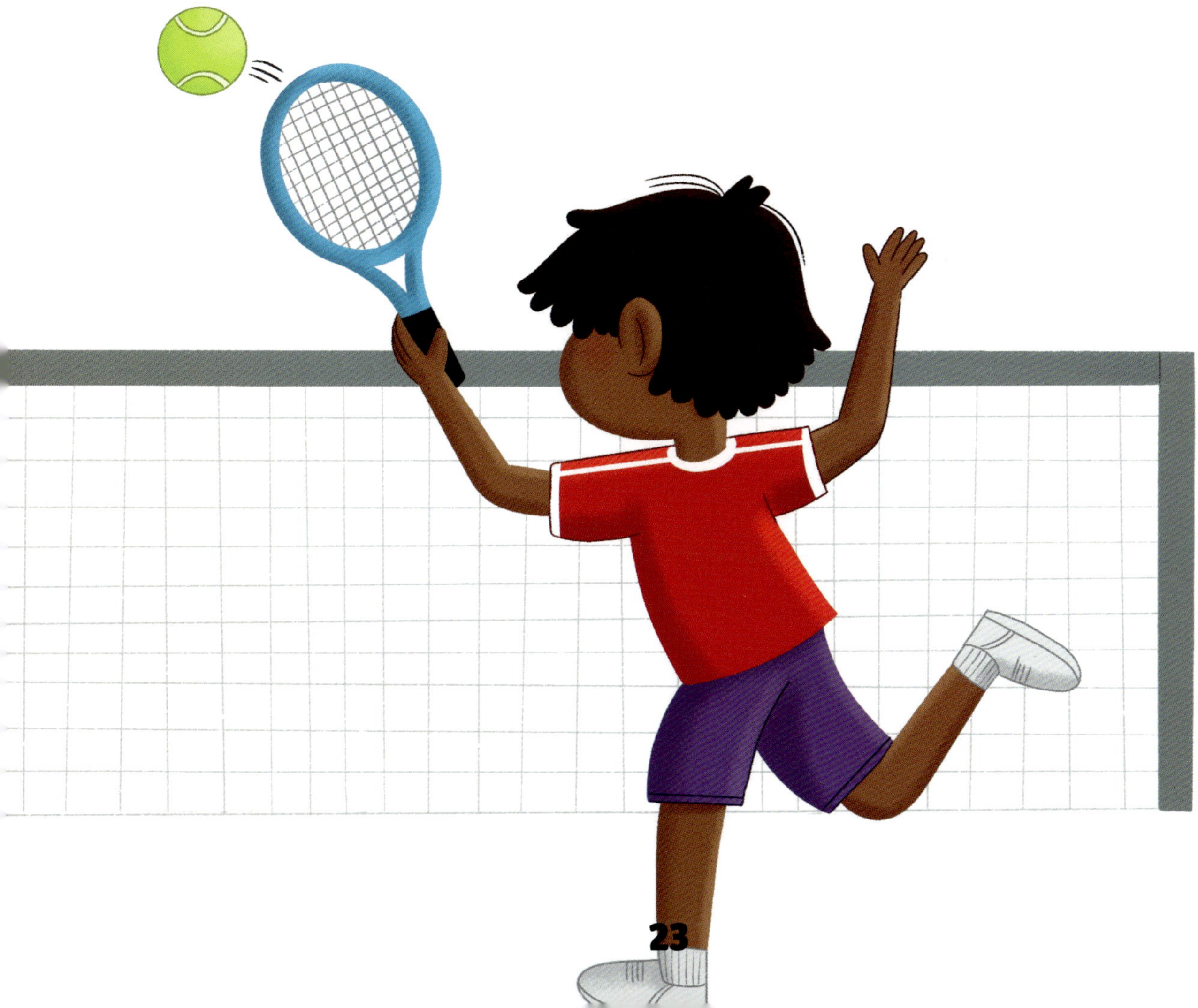

# CRANE

Cranes are much bigger machines than the machines we've looked at so far. Cranes are used in building to move very heavy loads.

They are much more complex than a simple see-saw, but they work the same way – they are levers.

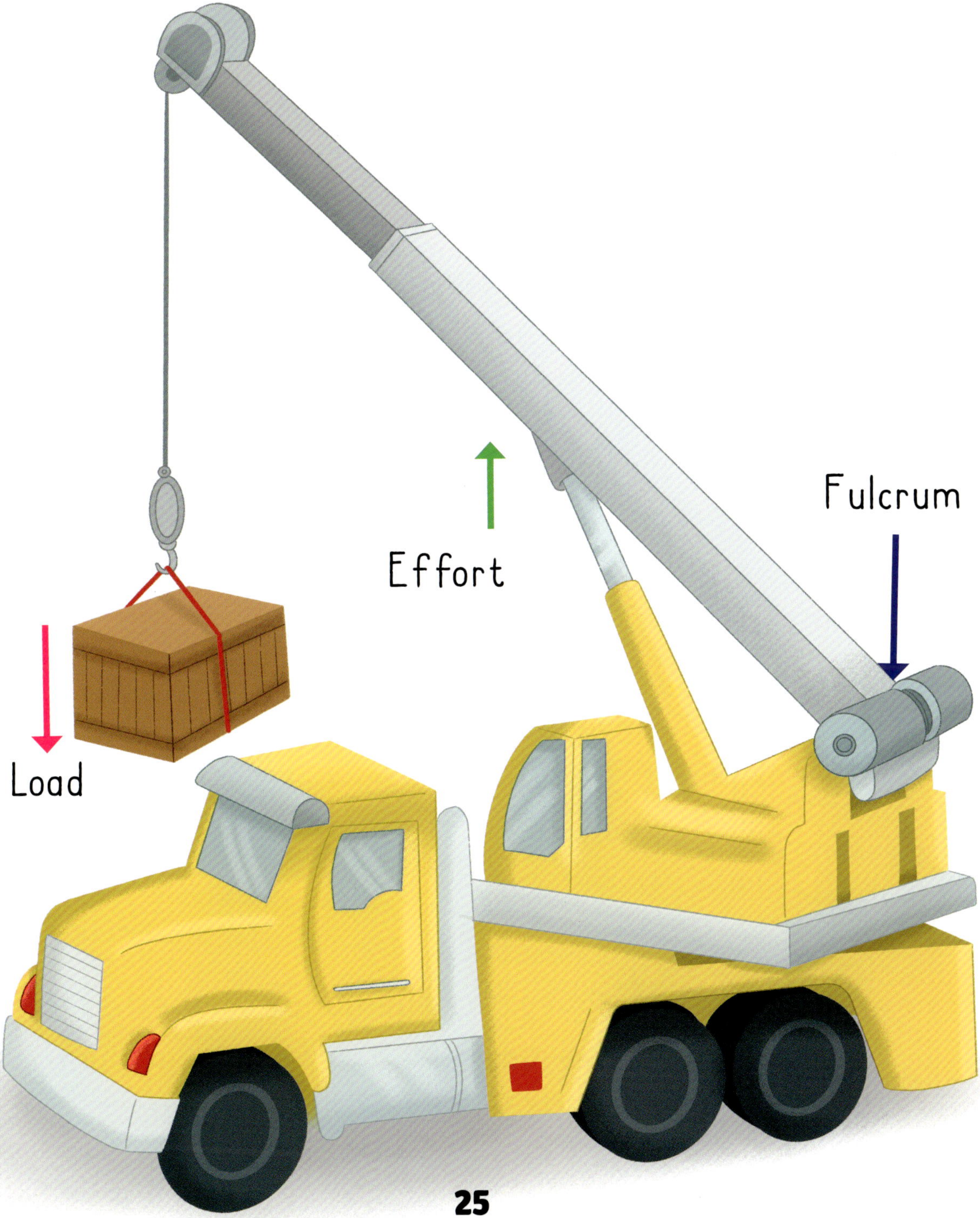
Effort
Fulcrum
Load

# LEVERS IN PAIRS: SCISSORS AND TWEEZERS

Scissors are a pair of levers hinged at the fulcrum.

The effort of squeezing the handles together slices through the material as they are pushed together. The load is the resistance of the material being cut.

Tweezers are also a pair of levers. You squeeze them in the middle. Tweezers are an example of a lever that makes it easy to lift or remove something that is not a heavy load.

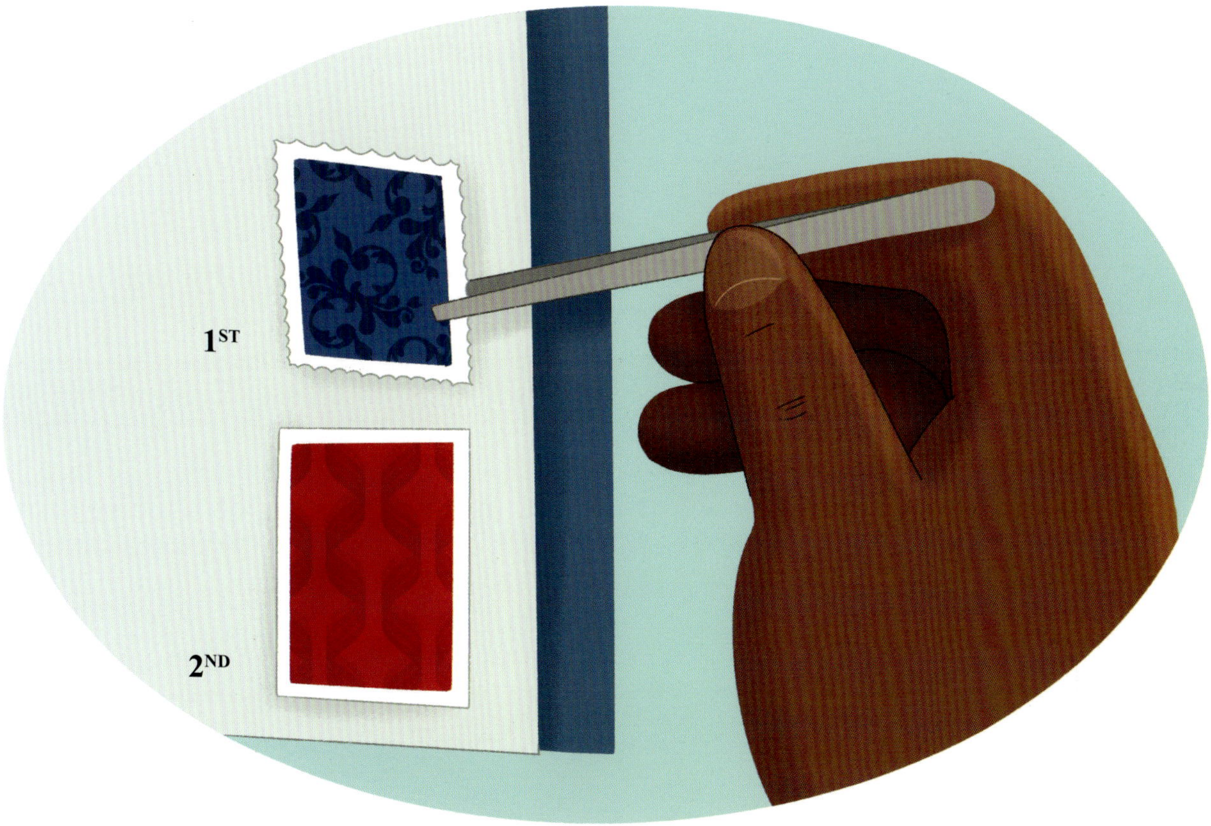


Can you think of any others?

# LEVERS AND PEOPLE

People have been using levers since the Stone Age, when they discovered that rocks they could not lift or push could be moved using branches as levers.

Did you know the ancient Egyptians used levers to build the pyramids?

Today, we use levers in many different ways.

We can use them to produce a big force over a short distance, as with scissors, or to produce a small force over a big distance, like a crane.

# GLOSSARY

Here are the key words we explored in this book. Try covering the meanings to see if you can remember them yourself. Were you right?

**Complex** having many different and connected parts.

**Force** a push or a pull.

**Fulcrum** the point on which the lever turns to lift a load. It is also called a pivot.

**Gravity** a pulling force. The gravity of Earth pulls things down.

**Lever** a machine that reduces the amount of force needed to move an object or lift a load.

**Load** this is the part that the lever moves, such as the soil in this wheelbarrow.

**Machine** anything that helps us by taking a force and transferring it to where it is needed.

**Muscles** the parts of your body which, with your bones, help you to move.

**Resistance** a stopping effect that one material has on another.

**Squeeze** pushing things together.

**Weight** the heaviness of a person or thing.

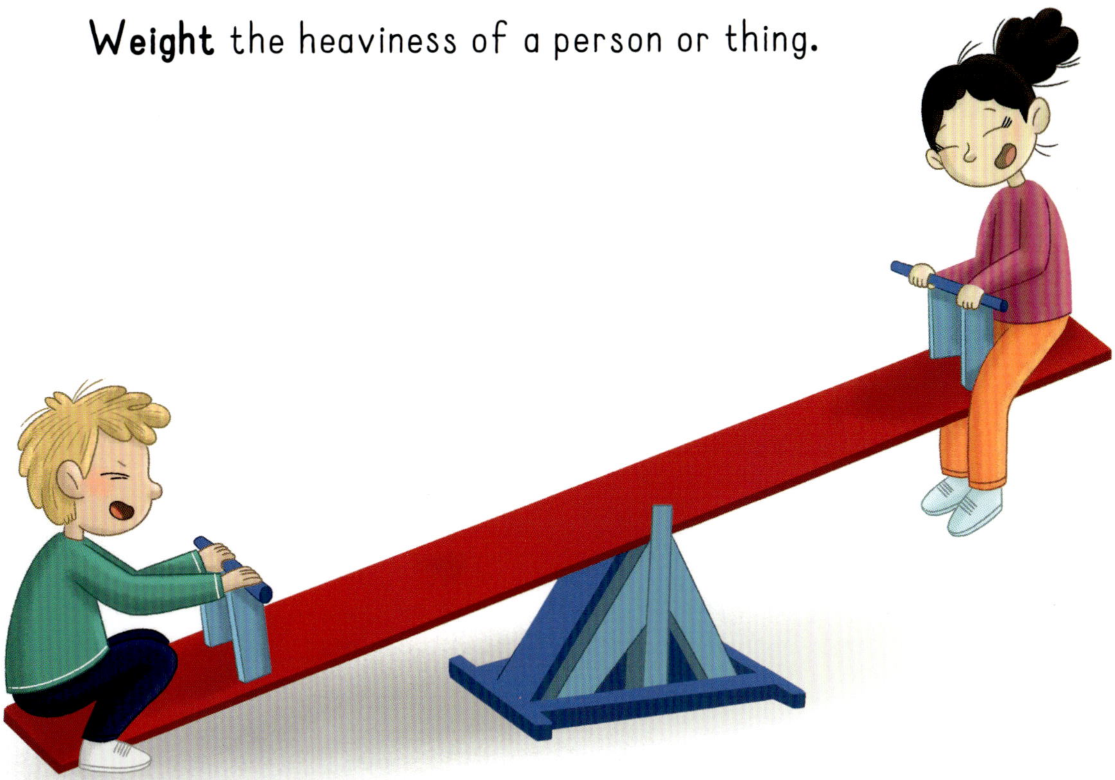

# INDEX



**Answer to question on page 5:** the six levers are the door, nail cutters, scissors, stapler, tennis racket, and tweezers. See if you can spot them all!